Animal Babies

Puppies

by Meg Gaertner

FOCUS READERS

SCOUT

www.focusreaders.com

Focus Readers is distributed by North Star Editions:
sales@northstareditions.com | 888-417-0195

Produced for Focus Readers by Red Line Editorial.

Photographs ©: Bigandt_Photography/iStockphoto, cover, 1; crisserbug/iStockphoto, 4; VioletaStoimenova/iStockphoto, 7 (top); kukiatB/iStockphoto, 7 (bottom); Anna Hoychuk/ Shutterstock Images, 9, 16 (top left), 16 (bottom left); Andrew Yates/Shutterstock Images, 11, 16 (top right); cmannphoto/iStockphoto, 13 (top); Photology1971/iStockphoto, 13 (bottom), 16 (bottom right); Peopleimages/iStockphoto, 15

Library of Congress Cataloging-in-Publication Data
Names: Gaertner, Meg, author.
Title: Puppies / by Meg Gaertner.
Description: Lake Elmo, MN : Focus Readers, [2020] | Series: Animal babies | Audience: K to Grade 3. | Includes index.
Identifiers: LCCN 2018060035 (print) | LCCN 2018061647 (ebook) | ISBN 9781641859578 (PDF) | ISBN 9781641858885 (ebook) | ISBN 9781641857505 (hardcover) | ISBN 9781641858199 (paperback)
Subjects: LCSH: Puppies--Juvenile literature.
Classification: LCC SF426.5 (ebook) | LCC SF426.5 .G335 2020 (print) | DDC 636.7/07--dc23
LC record available at https://lccn.loc.gov/2018060035

Printed in the United States of America
Mankato, MN
May, 2019

About the Author

Meg Gaertner is a children's book editor and author. She lives in Minneapolis, Minnesota. When not writing, she is usually dancing or spending time outside.

Table of Contents

eye
ear

First Days

Puppies are baby dogs.
A mother has
many puppies.
Their **eyes** are closed.
Their **ears** are closed.

Puppies stay with
their mother.
They drink her milk.
They sleep.

mother

Changes

Puppies open their eyes.

They can see.

Puppies open their ears.

They can hear.

ear
eye

Puppies stand.

They walk.

They wag their **tails**.

tail

Puppies grow **teeth**.

They eat solid food.

They play.

food

teeth

Growing Up

Puppies keep growing.

They find new homes.

They live with people.

Glossary

ears

tails

eyes

teeth

Index